A Book About Turtles

CREATURES ALL AROUND US

What's Under That Shell?

by D. M. Souza

 Carolrhoda Books, Inc./Minneapolis

Library of Congress Cataloging-in-Publication Data

Souza, D. M. (Dorothy M.)
  What's under that shell? / by D. M. Souza.
    p.   cm—(Creatures all around us)
  Includes index.
  Summary: Examines the characteristics, life cycle, and habitat of the turtle.
  ISBN 0-87614-712-0
  1. Turtles—Juvenile literature. [1. Turtles.] I. Title.
II. Series: Souza, D. M. (Dorothy M.). Creatures all around us.
QL666.C5S64   1992
597.92—dc20   91-32349
                                                  CIP
                                                   AC

Manufactured in the United States of America

1 2 3 4 5 6 7 8 9 10 01 00 99 98 97 96 95 94 93 92

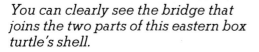
You can clearly see the bridge that joins the two parts of this eastern box turtle's shell.

What's Under That Shell?

Imagine a coat of armor strong enough to stop the teeth of an alligator. That is what some turtles have. But just as you cannot slip out of your skin whenever you wish to, a turtle can never slip out of its shell.

A turtle's shell has two parts—an upper part known as a **carapace** (KAR-uh-puhs) and a lower one called a **plastron** (PLAS-truhn). The two are joined on either side by a bony hinge, or bridge.

Both parts of the shell are made of bony material that is really part of the turtle's ribs and backbone. On top of this bony material is a layer of horny shields, or **scutes** (SKOOTZ). The scutes are similar to the scales of a snake or a lizard and come in many different colors and patterns. They are as different in each turtle as fingerprints are in humans.

Some turtles shed their outer scutes each year. Others grow new scutes that pile up on top of the old ones. Sometimes it is possible to find out how old a turtle is by counting its piled-up scutes, if they have not worn off.

Most turtles' shells are covered with scutes.

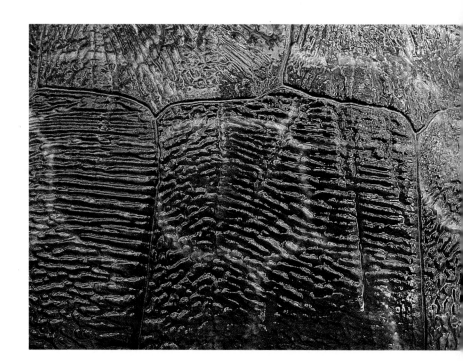

Soft-shelled turtles have soft, floppy shells.

A few kinds of freshwater turtles have shells that are soft and floppy. In place of scutes, they have a leathery skin that protects them. These turtles are called softshells.

Even though hard shells protect turtles, they do not let them move around easily. Turtles cannot bend in different directions the way we can. Only their heads, necks, legs, and tails can move freely.

Many turtles are slow-moving. Tortoises are the slowest of all reptiles. They can take almost four hours to travel a mile. But sea turtles are much faster. When frightened, loggerheads, which may weigh nearly a thousand pounds, can swim 18 to 20 miles an hour.

An eastern box turtle pulls its head into its shell.

The skin covering a turtle's head, neck, and legs is scaly and wrinkled. It is very loose, especially around the neck. This makes it possible for the reptile to stretch out its neck or pull it back into its shell. From time to time, some turtles shed their scaly skin the same way they shed their scutes.

6

This southern painted turtle has webbed feet, which help it move around in water.

The shape of a turtle's feet give hint of its **habitat** (HA-buh-tat), the place where it lives. Most turtles that live in streams, ponds, and lakes have webbed feet like a duck's. **Tortoises** (TORT-uh-suhz), turtles that live on land, have thick legs and feet like an elephant's. Sea turtles have legs in the form of flippers.

Turtles can see very well at short distances, but they cannot see things far away. They have no ears, but "hear" vibrations along the ground or in the water. Their sense of smell is strong, especially when food is nearby. Snapping turtles and other freshwater turtles can locate food even in the dark.

7

All turtles, even those that live in water, breathe air. When you inhale, your chest expands to make room for air entering your lungs. But a turtle's chest cannot expand. Instead, special muscles must push air in and out of its lungs.

Fortunately turtles do not need to breathe as often as we do. Some take only one breath an hour. Green turtles can stay underwater for as long as five hours without coming to the surface for air.

Turtles, like other reptiles, are **ectothermic** (ek-tuh-THUR-mik), or cold-blooded. Their temperatures rise or fall with the temperature of the air or water around them. If it gets cold, turtles must hide in a sheltered place or find a patch of sunlight in order to keep warm.

This spotted turtle is raising its body temperature by basking in the sun.

There are about 250 different kinds of turtles living in the warm parts of the world today. Some, such as the box turtle, weigh only a few ounces, or about as much as a plum. Others, such as the giant sea turtles, weigh over 1,500 pounds—as much as a truckload of watermelons. Usually, female turtles are larger than males. Female soft-shelled turtles can be two or three times larger than males.

Most turtles live longer than other animals, including humans. Scientists know of one tortoise that actually survived for 152 years. That's a long time to carry around a heavy coat of armor.

Galapagos tortoises can weigh as much as 500 pounds.

Male tortoises often bite females on the legs before mating with them.

Be Mine

Two tortoises are standing a short distance apart on the desert sand. The smaller of them, the male, grunts and stretches out his head and neck. As he approaches the female, she pulls her head and feet into her shell and peeks out. He bobs his head up and down in front of her. He is letting her know he wants to mate.

Several times, he tries to coax her out of hiding by bumping the side of her shell with his carapace. He even tries to bite the edge of her shell. But she keeps her head and legs tightly tucked within her shell.

11

Another male tortoise appears, and in minutes, a battle for the female begins. Both males pull their heads into their shells and bump against each other. Again and again their shells bang together with great force until one male flips the other one over on his back. As the upside-down turtle struggles to right himself, the challenger moves out of sight with the female. Soon they mate, then go their separate ways.

Many turtles behave in unusual ways during mating season. The giant tortoises that live on the Galapagos Islands off the west coast of South America grunt so loudly when trying to attract females that they can be heard for almost a mile. If two 300-pound males fight over the same female, you can be sure they make quite a rumble.

Male Galapagos tortoises bellow loudly during courtship and mating.

A male desert tortoise bumps a female to let her know he wants to mate with her.

When male and female snapping turtles meet, they do a face-to-face dance with each other near the surface of the water. They move their heads from side to side in opposite directions for several minutes. Then they stop and stare at one another, almost nose to nose.

Male and female wood turtles also swing their heads from side to side when they meet. This may go on for as long as two hours. They sometimes make noises that sound like the whistle of a teapot.

A male painted turtle may swim in circles around a female. He may swim backwards in front of her face and stretch out his front legs toward her. With his long claws, he tickles her head and cheeks.

Spotted turtles may chase wildly after females and thrash the water. Some sea turtles do a delicate ballet together. Each species (SPEE-sheez), or kind, of turtle has a special way of trying to win a mate.

Most turtles mate in spring and early summer. When the female is ready to lay her eggs, she begins searching for a place to hide them.

This male eastern box turtle is about to mate with the female underneath him.

A female eastern box turtle lays her eggs.

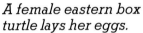

The Nest

It is late afternoon, and several painted turtles are sunning themselves on a log in the middle of the pond. Their shells are smooth and dark, and their heads, necks, and legs are streaked with yellow and red. All are about 6 inches long.

One female slips into the water, catches an insect, puts her head underwater, and swallows. Another female swims toward the edge of the pond, crawls out, and heads up the bank. She is ready to lay her eggs. Like all turtles, she will do this on land.

Predators found this snapping turtle nest and ate the eggs.

A few yards from the water, she stops in a sunny spot and begins digging with her hind legs. She digs a hole and covers it without laying any eggs. She may dig several holes and do the same thing. These false nests sometimes fool skunks, badgers, squirrels, raccoons, and other **predators** (PREH-duh-turz) that hunt for the turtle's eggs.

After about an hour of digging, the female finally lays six yellow-white eggs in one of the holes. When she is finished, she carefully covers them with soil or leaves, using her legs and lower shell to smooth the dirt. Heat from the sun and from rotting leaves on top of the nest will warm the eggs and help the developing young, or **embryos** (EM-bree-ohz), grow.

Female turtles, like many reptiles, never return to their eggs after laying them. Predators frequently find the eggs. This is why fewer than half of them ever hatch.

Each summer, female turtles of all types look for sunny spots on land where they can dig their nests. Tortoises and sea turtles usually hollow out places in the sand. Box turtles may dig holes in hay fields or in piles of decaying leaves. The holes may be a few inches deep or several feet, depending upon the size of the turtle.

A snapping turtle laid these eggs in a nest of soil.

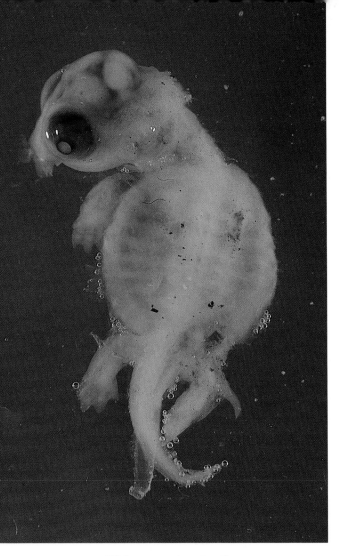

This snapping turtle embryo was removed from its egg before it was fully developed.

Different types of turtles lay different numbers of eggs. Spotted turtles, for example, lay 3 or 4 eggs, while snapping turtles lay 80 or more. The larger the turtle, the more eggs it lays. Turtle eggs may be shaped like a hen's or may look like ping-pong balls or tennis balls.

As the embryo develops within the egg, its body swells. After two or three months, it is so big that the egg breaks. A special egg tooth on the upper jaw and tiny claws on the front feet help the young turtle, or **hatchling**, get out of its shell.

A spiny softshell hatchling breaks out of its egg.

All the hatchlings begin digging their way out of their nest at about the same time. Their shells are soft, and if the young do not find a safe place, birds and other predators will make a meal of them. Many hatchlings die this way.

Those that escape danger stay in hiding until their shells harden. Small turtles become adults in 5 to 10 years, but larger ones take longer. After they mature, the turtles mate and females begin their own nest-building and egg-laying.

When this young snapping turtle is full-grown, it will weigh 30 to 60 pounds.

Toothless

On the bottom of a pond, half-buried in mud, is a large moss-covered object. It looks like a rock, but it is really a snapping turtle. It spends almost all of its time in the water.

Snappers are among the largest freshwater turtles in North America. They usually weigh about 30 to 60 pounds, and their shells look too small for their bodies.

20

Snapping turtles have strong, sharp beaks.

With eyes that sit close to the top of its head, the snapper watches a fish swim close by. As the fish circles, the turtle slowly stretches out its long neck and grabs its victim, or **prey** in its jaws. Before swallowing, it uses its hooked beak to cut the food into bite-sized chunks.

Once in a while, when a young duck lands on the surface of a pond, a snapping turtle will swim under it, grab it by the legs, and take it to the bottom of the pond for a feast. Like several other kinds of turtles, snappers do their eating underwater.

While waiting for food, the alligator snapping turtle sometimes uses a trick to attract prey. In the middle of its tongue is a long, thin piece of pink flesh. When the turtle holds its mouth open, this flesh looks like a squirming worm. A hungry fish spots it, swims too close, and snap! The turtle has a meal.

Turtles are toothless, but their jaws are strong and sharp. Many have edges like those of a saw. With them the reptiles can crunch snails and other hard-shelled creatures. Some turtles also have long claws that help them rip food apart.

Look closely and you'll see the special piece of pink flesh on this alligator snapper's tongue.

Turtles eat a variety of things depending upon their size and where they live. Tortoises eat plants and flowers, so they are said to be **herbivorous** (er-BIH-vuh-ruhs). Some turtles chomp on fish, shellfish, snails, or insects. They are meat-eating, or **carnivorous** (kar-NIH-vuh-ruhs). Many turtles are **omnivorous** (ahm-NIH-vuh-ruhs), meaning they eat both plants and animals. Some also eat the bodies of dead animals that they find.

23

The green turtle, an ocean dweller, has raised ridges on the roof of its mouth. These help the reptile grab clumps of grasses growing on the ocean floor. The green turtle also likes to eat jellyfish and sponges.

All turtles are able to go for long periods without food. Some can live for almost a year without eating, but most like to eat as often as they can.

Turtles drink water regularly. Those that live in dry places get much of their water from the plants they eat. Some tortoises are able to store water in their bodies in special places called **cloacal** (klo-AY-kuhl) **bladders**. This makes it possible for them to go for long periods without a fresh water supply.

This smooth softshell has a round, flat shell.

Winter and Summer Burrows

A strange-looking turtle walks along the muddy river bottom. The shell on its back is round and flat like a pancake. It is floppy, not hard like the shells of other turtles, and it is covered with leathery skin instead of horny shields. This is a soft-shelled turtle.

26

With its stretched-out neck and tube-like nose, the softshell turns over stone after stone. Now and again it finds an insect, worm, or crayfish under a stone and swallows it whole. The weather has turned cool, and the softshell will soon look for a safe place to hide.

Once it finds a sheltered spot, the softshell will use the edge of its shell to work its way under the mud. When its entire body is covered, it will rest. Not until warm weather returns will it move out of hiding.

Animals that go into hiding during the winter are said to **hibernate** (HY-buhr-nayt). Usually turtles go into hibernation gradually. Late in the day a turtle may bury itself in a few inches of mud or fallen leaves. The next day, when the sun shines, it will leave its hideout and warm itself in the sun.

Soft-shelled turtles, such as this Florida softshell, have long, tube-like noses.

As the weather gets colder each night, the turtle will bury itself deeper and deeper under cover. The box turtle, for example, may begin hiding in a hole 2 inches deep. But by the time winter arrives, the hole will be 8 or 10 inches below the ground. During hibernation, the turtle stops eating, and its breathing slows.

Different types of turtles find different places to hide. Painted turtles, snapping turtles, and softshells look for mud at the bottom of a pond or stream. Stinkpots and spotted turtles sometimes move into abandoned muskrat houses, and wood turtles may dig holes in the side of a bank.

Some turtles go into hiding not only during winter but on hot summer days too. We say they **estivate** (ES-tuh-vayt) when they do this. Water turtles, for example, stay cool by wriggling into the muddy floors of ponds or streams that have little or no water in them. They stay there until rain falls again.

Desert tortoises that live in the western part of the United States dig two kinds of burrows to hide in. One is only a few feet deep, and the tortoises use it on the hottest days of summer. The other burrow may be 8 to 30 feet deep and is used during winter.

The winter burrow is usually dug in sandy or gravelly soil near a bush or at the bottom of a cliff for protection. The tortoise uses the thick claws on its front legs to scoop out the soil.

This hideout may be straight down or curved. It may have several passageways or contain one large room. Many tortoises may get together to dig and then move into the same burrow.

One way or another, turtles manage to escape weather that is too hot or too cold.

A gopher tortoise comes out of its winter burrow.

Loggerhead sea turtles are expert swimmers.

In the Sea

The largest turtles in the world can be found in the ocean. They are called sea turtles (or marine turtles). Leatherbacks, for example, are giants that can reach 8 feet in length and weigh 2,000 pounds—as much as some whales.

Sea turtles such as leatherbacks, loggerheads, green turtles, hawksbills, and ridleys are all expert swimmers. Their powerful flippers move them swiftly and gracefully through the water. Their large front flippers act as paddles, and the back ones do the steering.

The shells of sea turtles differ from those of other turtles. Leatherbacks, for example, have only rubbery skin that covers many small bones. Most sea turtles have only a thin layer of bone beneath their scutes instead of a thick one.

Sea turtles feed on anything they can find in the water. Their food may include underwater plants, clams, oysters, sea urchins, sponges, coral, or various kinds of fish. These turtles like to hunt in waters near shore. When they're not hunting, their favorite pastime is sunning themselves while floating on the surface of the water.

On summer nights, female sea turtles can be seen struggling onto beaches and searching for places to lay their eggs. They dig pits in the sand with all four flippers. Then they lay between 100 and 150 round eggs in the pits. Each female covers the hole with sand, rests for a few minutes, and returns to the sea. About 12 to 15 days later, several females may return, dig new holes, and lay more eggs.

Loggerhead hatchlings head back to the sea soon after they hatch.

Sea turtles lay 400 or more eggs in one season. They do not lay eggs every year as other turtles do, however. They usually lay them every two or three years.

The lives of sea turtles are constantly in danger. When they come ashore to lay their eggs, females are often attacked by predators. Their nests are robbed by dogs, raccoons, and even people. Frequently, baby sea turtles, like other turtle hatchlings, are snatched by predators soon after they hatch.

So many hawksbills have been killed for their shells, meat, and eggs that there are hardly any left.

Sea turtles are often caught in fishermen's nets or injured by boats. Thousands of green turtles have been hunted for their meat. Their shells, as well as those of hawksbills, are sometimes turned into tortoiseshell jewelry or used for household decorations.

Like sea turtles, other turtles have a hard time surviving in modern times. As streams, lakes, and ponds are drained to make room for buildings, turtles and their homes are destroyed.

Each year, hundreds of tortoises are hit by fast-moving cars while trying to cross roads. Many freshwater turtles are caught and eaten by people.

It's true that a turtle's armor has helped it survive for millions of years. But if these reptiles are going to continue to live for years to come, they will need quite a bit of help from you and your friends.

Scientists who study animals group them together according to their similarities and differences. Animals that have certain features in common are placed in the same groups. Turtles belong to the order, or group, of reptiles known as Testudines, or shelled reptiles. Within the order, there are many different families of turtles. Below are some of the members of the seven families of turtles that live in and around North America, along with a few facts about them.

FAMILY	EXAMPLES	SIZE IN INCHES	FAVORITE FOODS	HABITAT
Kinosternidae	mud turtles	3-7	snails, insects, small shellfish	shallow water, creeks, rivers, ponds, swamps, marshes
Chelydridae	snapping turtle	8-18	fish, water birds, plants, small mammals	all fresh water
Emydidae	wood turtle	5-9	water plants, berries, insects, slugs	woods, fields, bogs, swamps
	box turtles	4-8½	berries, plants, worms, snails	meadows, green woodlands, prairies
Testudinidae	desert tortoise	9-14	grasses, fruit	dry land, canyon bottoms, washes
Trionychidae	Florida softshell	5-19	snails, frogs, crayfish, fish	all fresh water
Cheloniidae	green turtles	28-60	water plants, jellyfish, sponges	open seas and coastlines
	hawksbill	30-36	seaweed, squid, octopi	shallow, rocky areas along coastlines

Glossary

carapace: the upper part of a turtle's shell

carnivorous: able to eat a diet of meat

cloacal bladders: places inside turtles' bodies where water is stored

ectothermic: having a body temperature that changes depending on the temperature of the environment

embryos: the young of an animal in the beginning stages of development

estivate: to spend the summer in a hiding place, in a sleeplike state

habitat: the place where a type of animal lives

hatchling: a newborn animal such as a turtle

herbivorous: able to eat a diet of plants

hibernate: to spend the winter in a hiding place, in a sleeplike state

omnivorous: able to eat a diet of both plants and animals

plastron: the lower part of a turtle's shell

predators: animals that hunt and eat other animals

prey: animals that are killed and eaten by other animals

scutes: bony shields on the outside of a turtle's shell

tortoises: turtles that live on land

Index

The photographs are reproduced through the courtesy of: pp. 1 (left), 3, 31, 33, 34, © Connie Toops; pp. 1 (right), 6, 20, © Tom Cawley; pp. 4, 22, © James C. Godwin; pp. 5, 7, 9, 16, 19, 21, 23, 29, 36, back cover, Allen Blake Sheldon; pp. 10, 12, © R. E. Barber 1991; p. 11, Eda Rogers/Sea Images; p. 13, Animals Animals © 1991 Zig Leszczynski; pp. 14, 15, 23, 37, © Joe McDonald; pp. 17, 18, Dwight R. Kuhn; pp. 25, 35, © Franklin and Kathy Viola; p. 26, © Dan Nedrelo; pp. 27, 30, front cover, © J. H. Robinson. Turtle illustration courtesy of Darren Erickson.